TRESCO

ABBEY GARDEN

Tresco Abbey Garden, Tresco, Isles of Scilly, Cornwall, TR24 OPU. www.tresco.co.uk
open daily 10.00 - 4.00

Published by Truran 2004. Truran is an imprint of Truran Books Ltd,
Croft Prince, Mount Hawke, Truro, Cornwall. TR4 8EE. www.truranbooks.co.uk

Printed & bound in Cornwall by R Booth Ltd, Antron Hill, Mabe, Penryn
Cornwall. TR10 9HH.

ISBN   1   85022 186 3

into the garden ~ & into a world completely separate from the seasons & the weather outside. Bamboos, olive trees, exotic foliage, bright flowers at any time of year..

Rosemary, lavender, olive trees, spiky things - layer after layer of light & dark, brightness & shadow

A wonderful spot to sit near the entrance. shaded on a hot July day. Birds singing, water falling gently. It's hard to believe that this is one of the newer parts of the garden. It's full of lush growth, tumbling flowers - & big spiky things. I'm sorry but I always get their names mixed up, but as soon as I sat down I loved the way the fountain was echoed by a real, spiky palm thing behind.

4

Chilean Wine Palm & Norfolk Island Pine

5

the Neptune steps - Tall trunks & enormously tall hedge framing the view

Huge flower spikes from spiky plants.
Some deep bright red, lime green flowers

8 Beschorneria

Puya

some tall, bright yellow green with
yellow flowers. Blackbirds drinking yesterdays rain
from the Puya flowers.

9

I don't mind sharing my lunch with a few sparrows... but I draw the line at a large, pushy pheasant...

The cock pheasant is far too dignified to pick crumbs from my table... He simply poses for photographs...

fallen petals, flowering herbs
r a chat with the ducks

11

Two urns on the Neptune steps

These original lattice work pots were designed specially for here by Augustus Smith

12

every bench has a wonderful view - olive trees & fountain from here

this bench is a garden on its own - completely covered with pale, soft lichen.

13

A Monet painting - only living & changing, with birds bathing & disturbing the surface. Shadows passing & children laughing....

I wish I were an Impressionist.

14

Garden landmarks - the Archway - always seems to be light r onger
And Grand - Massively
  beautiful - r so
hard to get her
proportions right

15

Flowering Aloes

16

very tall Agave flower spike

im sorry this has to be this
way up... there was just no other →
way it would fit
it must be nearly 20i high....

17

18 pin cushion protea

King Protea - smells of rubber to me - very odd. 19

There is a garden within the garden. Looking beyond all the
dramatic trees, spiky plants & strange foliage...

Pincushion Protea - Scarlet ribbons they all look like flowers designed to be the most artificial & exotic ones around. They even smell peculiar! but they are spectacularly beautiful... & very difficult to draw...

and this is the very opposite of the showy proteas..
I always notice the bright orange/red berries of the stinking Iris.. &
this year I've searched for the flowers & found them hiding in

undergrowth, pale & unobtrusive —
& very delicate & beautiful

20

...looking down & looking closer...

tiny, tumbling, delicate flowers
on a shrub near the abbey
arch...

dark pink/mauve spots
on the pale mauve.
warmer/more orange
spots on the yellow
—comes from Chile.

The inside of
this protea is soft & furry,
like some kind of small animal—
not a plant.

watched by sparrows,
a chaffinch bathing,
a blackbird singing just for me.

21

... there are endless strange flowers & scents

can't read the label on this one

pink columbian passion Flowers

Tropical American Morning Glory

can't read this one either but it comes from Australia

these tiny flowers' petals cover the ground under a big tree with delicate leaves..

october - it has a big seed

Bees visiting the flowers

cobaea scandeus
polemoniaceae

mexico

v. pale yellow green
stems r v slightly
yellower buds
lots of ants among
the flowers

Don't know what this is *.
Its growing up the terrace by the Shell house
I've drawn the flower about ½ life size. Its a vine-like
plant - the new leaves r shoots are a deep maroon/
purple.. wonderful! * Its called cup r saucer vine...
r is south American

23

I think this is some
kind of eucalyptus
a pinker kind of pink
than the bottlebrush

Yes it is because
heres a small
white one

the bottle brush always makes me smile
its such a ridiculous sort of flower

24

Chilean Bell Flower

Bomarea Caldasii — climber from Brazil

growing in amongst evergreen hedge

this looks like a Fuschia but is very fleshy... it is a kind of Fuschia

a single flower from a huge spike

25

MidMay - the garden is
full of echiums. Their
colours range from pale,
cool blue with paler pink
centres to the deepest
mauve/cobalt with
bright pink stamens.
All full of bees . .

The flowers grow in spirals
round the stem. Sometimes
spaced thinly & sometimes
clustered so that the stems
cannot be seen . .

The garden all pink &
purple & blue

furry centres
growing in a spiral
towards the centre.

pale pinky grey
underneath

wiry yellow
stamens
with furry
orange/ochre
tops.

Agapanthus
such an impossible
colour...
such a beautiful flower.

27

I don't think I can
convey the shock of the
colours on this Puya...
lime green stems, rich blue green
flowers & bright orange stamens.

silvery 'furry buds

silvery undersides to leaves.

im sitting in the shade of a
mimosa type tree, surrounded
by the pale trunks of gum
trees, dappled with mauve,
grey shadows.
Peaceful & cool here on
a very hot early June day...

Blackbirds are sitting on the
spikes of blossom & drinking from the flowers...

seed heads & dying flowers from rush type things in the pond!

prehistoric-looking seedpods of the New Zealand Flax

29

Kauri Pine — one of the giant forest trees of the world.

After the gales...

The grass is littered with leaves & branches.

Stinkwoods

Pitcairn Bromeliad

31

Isoplexus from the Canaries

Scilla Peruviana?

Datura - & a wild hogweed
exotic & ordinary - both beautiful.

Bush echium

Abutilon - my very favourite

Marguerites

Dragon Arum - hidden in the leaves & grasses

33

Lampranthus in every shade of pink

seagulls above the trees...
the only thing to remind you
about the world outside!..

first Belladonnas in with the last Agapanthus

old pots

new ones

36

37

Harvesting Agapanthus -
bright cobalt, mauve growing in amongst the brightest purple heath
I've ever seen.

Had to get here really early this morn
they start picking out in the dunes at
about 8am.

38

The flowers are harvested out here because those grown in the garden are so huge that they won't fit in the flower boxes! '39

Mike packing flowers

Agapanthus everywhere.
small black cats playing in the
flower boxes

well he didn't
stay there long —
He's now jumping
on my lap!....
ouch...

OZ.

OLLIE

This one's a bit quieter

40

compost, compost
& more compost

41

The Eucalyptus trees are festooned with streamers of bark. Do they do this every year?

42.

love their pale, ghostly trunks. Hot. wind getting up now & blowing 43
in hazy grey cloud.

44   Nikau Palm,   Black Tree Fern,   Bananas.

bbage Tree

Chusan Palm

ere are lots of things I love about this garden
ut all the exotic foliage - & its shadows -
as to be the best

45

Euphorbia - it looks like
a cactus to me. -

46

Phoenix Canariensis

Butia

47

it's not till you get to the very top of the garden that you remember
There's a big world out There... Islands, rocks, choppy seas —
& its time to go back to reality & the boat home

48